For Tim and Joe for all their help

First published in Great Britain in 2002 by Zero To Ten Limited
327 High Street, Slough, Berkshire, SL1 1TX

Publisher: Anna McQuinn
Art Director: Tim Foster
Senior Editor: Simona Sideri
Publishing Assistant: Vikram Parashar

Copyright © 2002 Zero to Ten Limited
Photographs copyright © 2002 Sally Smallwood

A CIP catalogue record for this book is available from the British Library.

ISBN 1-84089-228-5

Printed in Hong Kong

Picture credits
A-Z Botanical Collection: coconut; Holt Studios: banana, sultanas, strawberry;
Photos Horticultural: kiwi fruit, apple, lemon; Pictor: pineapple.

Sally Smallwood

Sweet as a Strawberry!

pineapple

chunk

chunk

slice

chunk

sweet

leaf

prickly skin

kiwi fruit

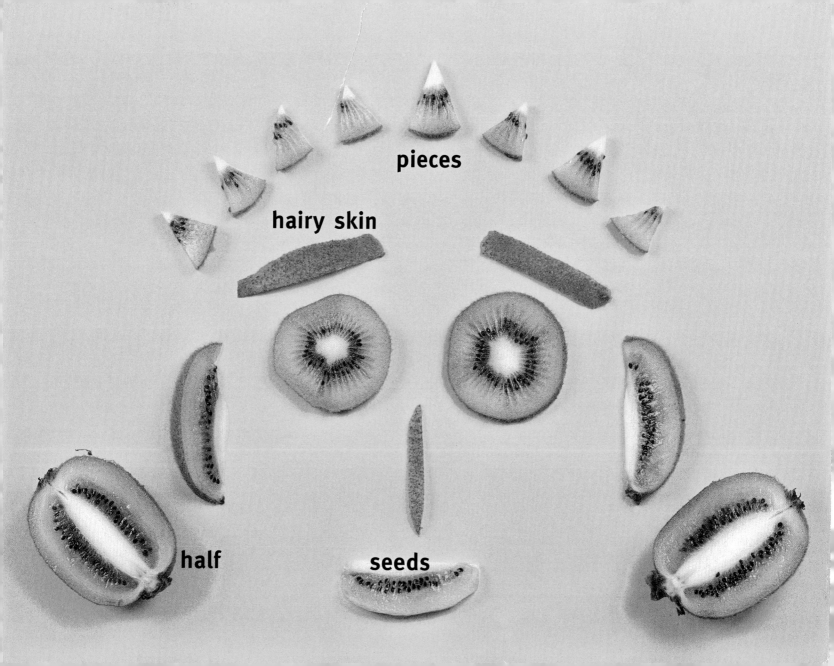

pieces

hairy skin

half

seeds

banana

sultanas

creamy and smooth like...

mashed potatoes

pear

mango

chewy and tasty like...

corn on the cob

dried apricots

bagel

black grapes

bunches

currants: dried black grapes

white grapes

skin

half

sultanas: dried white grapes

coconut

dry and tasty like...

  lentils

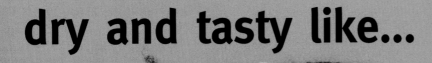

popcorn

hairy shell

pieces

coconut water

sweet

large piece

apple

crunchy and sweet like...

watermelon

corn on the cob

red pepper

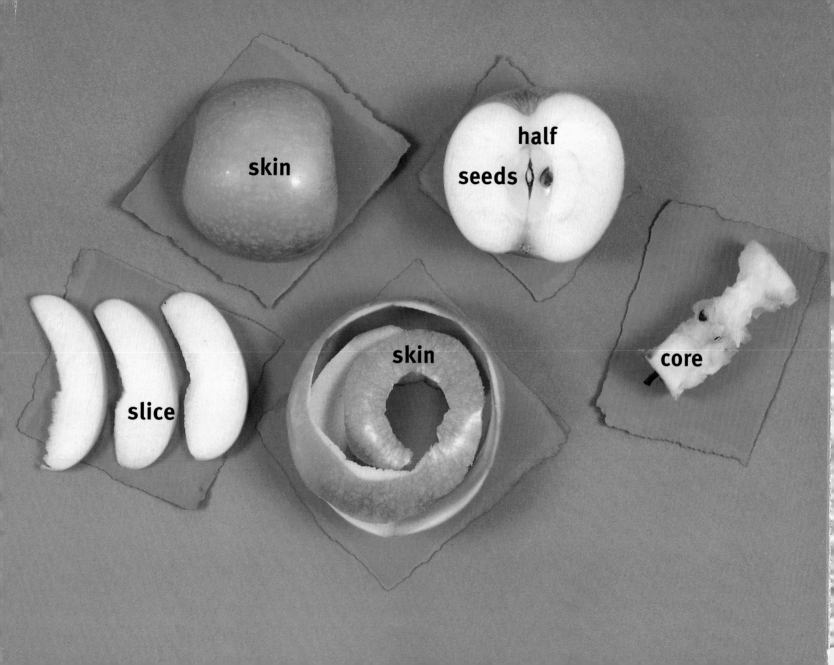

strawberry

lemon

sweet and sour like...

juicy

peel

quarter pieces

slices

slice